100 WORDS
Kids Need to Read by 1st Grade

Sight word practice to build strong readers

from the editors of Scholastic News

Scholastic
Professional Books

New York • Toronto • London • Auckland • Sydney

Contents

3...My 100 Words to Read

Group 1
4...Find the Word
5...Word Math
6...Match It!
7...What Am I?

Group 2
8...Who Am I?
9...Which Word?
10...Which Way Is Up?
11...Mystery Letter

Group 3
12...Read and Spell
13...Yes or No?
14...My Good Friend
15...Match It!

Group 4
16...Which Word?
17...Match It!
18...Friends Share
19...Rhyming Pear Tree

Group 5
20...Go Car, Go!
21...This or That?
22...What Am I?
23...Sort It Out!

Group 6
24...Letter Detective
25...How Many?
26...Sparky and Lisa's Day
31...If Numbers Were Walking

Mini Book
27...Balloons for Lilly

Dear Educator,

Teachers know and experts agree that the only way for children to master sight words—those high frequency, often non-decodable words essential to reading fluency—is through practice. With *100 Words Kids Need to Read*, we are pleased to offer a tool to help you provide that practice in an engaging, effective format.

We created the three books in this series—for first, second, and third graders—with the guidance of literacy experts and classroom teachers. Broken down into manageable groups, words are introduced in context and reinforced through inviting puzzles and games. Each sequence of activities is carefully designed to touch on reading, writing, and usage—taking children beyond mere visual recognition of sight words to genuine mastery.

The journey through these skill-building pages will help young readers make the successful transition from learning to read to reading to learn. Along the way, they will also receive excellent preparation for standardized tests. Enjoy the trip!

David Goddy
VP, Publisher

ANSWER KEY

Page 4: Words to be marked follow in bold: Lilly has **a** cat. **The cat is little** The cat goes **to** Lilly. **Page 5:** at; an; as. **Page 6:** From top to bottom, pictures match sentences 2, 1, 5, 4, 3. **Page 7:** hidden picture = panda in bamboo. **Page 8:** Answers will vary. **Page 9:** 1. play; 2. jump; 3. fast; 4. run; 5. ran. **Page 10:** 1. down; 2. out; 3. up; 4. on; 5. in. **Page 11:** 2. o; 3. p; 4. u; 5. n. **Page 12:** 2. father; 3. and; 4. were; 5. They. **Page 13:** Answers will vary. **Page 14:** friend; We; are; good. **Page 15:** From top, pictures match sentences 2, 3, 1. **Page 16:** 1. Will; 2. sit, sat; 3. ate; 4. be; 5. eat; 6. be, ate. **Page 17:** night; stop; day; rain. **Page 18:** went; with; of; for; from; If. **Page 19:** 2. night; 3. stop; 4. ate; 5. will; 6. sleep. **Page 31:** Number words to be circled appear as follows: verse 2: One; verse 3: One, Two, Two; verse 4: Two; verse 5: Two, Three, One, Two; verse 6: Four's; verse 7: Five, Ten; verse 8: Six, Five, Seven; verse 9: Seven; verse 10: Eight's; verse 11: Nine, Ten; verse 12: Ten, zero, one.

Page 20: go; look; 7. be; 8. sat; 9. went. **Page 21:** 2. that; saw; wants; can go; goes. **Page 22:** This; 3. old; 4. new; 5. hidden picture = flower. **Page 23:** Actions: see; saw, go; Things: book, car; Colors: blue, orange, green, red, yellow. **Page 24:** 1. o, a; 2. i, a; 3. e, o; u. **Page 25:** 1. two; 2. four; 3. three; 4. one. **Page 26:** 1. seven; 2. eight; 3. three; 4. five. **Mini Book:** rain; to; car; mother; with; has; seven; get; girl; two; gave; orange; He; to; They; play; as; good; sleep.

Editor: Kaaren Sorensen **Art Directors:** Joan Michael, Deborah Dinger, Vanessa Frazier, Beth Benzaquin **Editorial Consultants:** Wiley Blevins, Mary C. Rose, Sue Sxczepanski **Writers:** Laine Falk, Spencer Kayden, Jessica B. Levine **Copy Editors:** L.C. Israel, Bryan Brown **Production Editor:** Barbara Schwartz **Magazine Group:** VP, Publisher: David Goddy•VP, Editor in Chief: Rebecca Bondor•Associate Editorial Director: Alyse Sweeney•Design Director: Judith Christ-Lafond•Production Director: Barbara Schwartz•Executive Director of Photography: Steven Diamond•Publishing System Director: David Hendrickson•Manager, Digital Imaging Group: Marc Stern•Director of Library Service: Bert Schacter•Library Manager: Maggie Stevaralgia•VP, Marketing: Jocelyn Forman•**Scholastic Education**: President: Margery Mayer•Group VP Marketing: Greg Worrell• Director, Customer Service Technical Support: Karine Apollon-Mowatt• Associate Director of Customer Service: Pat Drayton

To order more issues or for customer service: 1- 800-SCHOLASTIC

Copyright © 2001 by Scholastic • All rights reserved. Published by Scholastic, Inc • Scholastic and associated logos are trademarked and/or registered trademarks of Scholastic Inc. No part of this publication may be reproduced, or stored in a retrieval system, or transmitted in any form or by any means, electronic, mechanical, photocopying, recording or otherwise, without written permission of the publisher. For information regarding permission, write to Scholastic Inc., Attention: Permissions Department, 557 Broadway, New York, NY 10012

Library of Congress Cataloging-in-Publications Data available ISBN 0-439-39929-7
40 39 38 37 36   25 26 Printed in the USA.   First printing X

My 100 Words to Read

Group 1

a	girl	little
an	goes	she
as	has	the
at	he	to
boy	is	was
by	it	

Group 2

am	jump	play
down	me	ran
fast	my	run
have	off	up
I	on	
in	out	

Group 3

and	friend	they
are	good	we
did	had	were
do	mother	yes
don't	no	you
father	not	

Group 4

ate	if	sit
be	look	stop
day	night	went
eat	of	will
for	rain	with
from	sat	

Group 5

black	green	see
blue	new	that
book	old	this
can	orange	want
car	red	yellow
go	saw	

Group 6

came	get	six
come	give	ten
eight	got	three
five	nine	two
four	one	
gave	seven	

Find the Word

Directions: Read the story. Then follow the directions below.

Lilly has a cat.
The cat is little.
The cat goes to Lilly.

1. Put a ⟨circle⟩ around the word **a**.

2. <u>Underline</u> the word **is**.

3. Put a |box| around the word **The** two times.

4. Put a ✓ over the word **little.**

5. Put a ★ over the word **goes.**

Word Math

Directions: Make new words by adding letters to the letter **a**. We did the first one for you.

1 a + t = <u>at</u>

2 a + n = _____

3 a + s = _____

Now circle the new words you made in the sentences below.

1 The girl is at home.

2 The boy has an apple.

3 The dog is as big as the girl.

Match It!

Directions: Draw a line from each sentence to the picture it matches. We did the first one for you.

1. He is a boy.

2. A girl has a little dog.

3. She is by the tree.

4. He goes to school.

5. It is an apple.

What Am I?

Directions: What kind of animal is hidden in this picture? Follow the directions to find out.

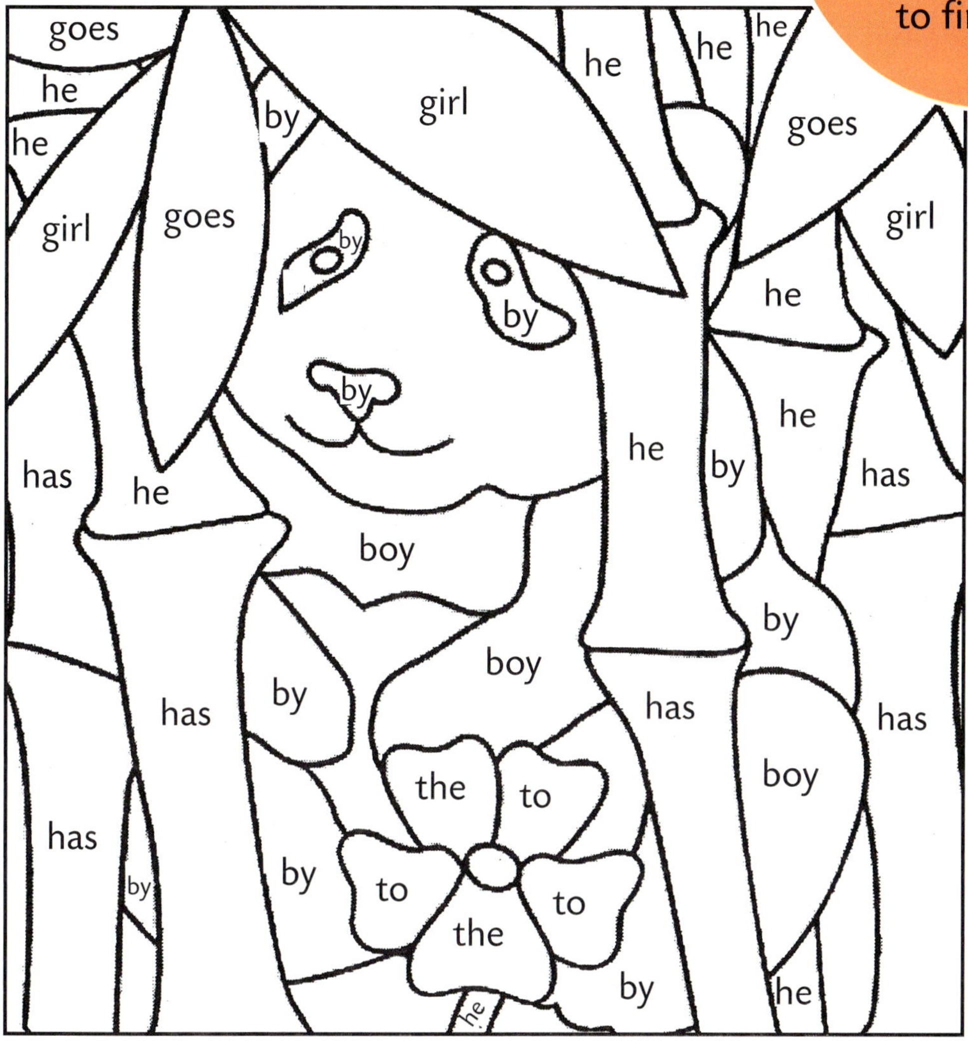

If the word starts with **t**, color the space

If the word starts with **h**, color the space

If the word starts with **g**, color the space

If the word starts with **b**, color the space

Who Am I ?

Directions: Read about Sam. Then answer the questions about you.

My name is Sam.
I am six years old.
I have brown hair.
This is a picture of me.

Now it is your turn.

My name is _____.

(Circle) one:

I am    years old.

I have     hair.

          black   **red**   **brown**   **blond**

This is a picture of me! (Draw a picture of yourself here.)

Which Word?

Directions: Read the story. Then answer each question with a blue word from the story. We did the first one for you.

My dog Pete can play.
He can jump.
He can run fast. I ran with Pete.

....

① Which blue word starts with **p**? ___play___

② Which blue word starts with **j**? _____

③ Which blue word rhymes with **last**? _____

④ Which blue word rhymes with **fun**? _____

⑤ Which blue word rhymes with **man**? _____

Which Way Is Up?

Directions: Look at each picture. Then ⓒircle the correct word for each sentence. Write the word on the line.

3

The cat runs _____ the tree.
up   down

1

The cat runs _____ the tree.
up   down

4

The cat is _____ the box.
on   off

2

The cat goes _____ of the box.
in   out

5

The cat is _____ the box.
on   in

Mystery Letter

Letter Box

u p ~~m~~ o n

Directions:
In each set of words, the same letter is missing. Can you find the mystery letter in each set? The letters you need are in the **Letter Box**. We did the first one for you.

1
_m_e
_m_y
ju_m_p
The mystery letter is _m_.

2
d____wn
____ff
____n
The mystery letter is ____.

3
u____
____lay
jum____
The mystery letter is ____.

4
____p
r____n
o____t
The mystery letter is ____.

5
ra____
i____
o____
The mystery letter is ____.

GROUP TWO

Read and Spell

Directions: Read the story, then put a ✓ next to the correct word that completes each sentence. Write the word on the line. We did the first one for you.

Sam's father went to the park. Sam and his mother were there. Sam played with his mother and father. They had a good time at the park.

1 Sam was at the park with his ___mother___.
___ muther
___ mohter
✓ mother

2 Sam saw his _____ at the park.
___ father
___ fahter
___ fother

3 Sam was with his mother _____ father.
___ an
___ nad
___ and

4 They _____ all at the park.
___ ware
___ wir
___ were

5 _____ played.
___ Thay
___ They
___ The

GROUP THREE

Yes or No?

Directions: Read the story. Then answer the questions. Circle your answers. Then write your answers on the lines.

Jen is a girl. Jen is six. Jen does not like bugs. Jen likes mud. Jen jumped in the mud. Are you like Jen?

1 Are you a girl?

_____ , I _____ a girl.

Yes   No   am   am not

2 Are you six?

_____ , I _____ six.

Yes   No   am   am not

3 Do you like bugs?

_____ , I _____ like bugs.

Yes   No   do   don't

4 Did you jump in the mud?

_____ , I _____ jump in the mud.

Yes   No   did   did not

5 Do you like mud?

_____ , I _____ like mud.

Yes   No   do   don't

GROUP THREE

My Good Friend

Directions: Use the words from the **Word Box** to write a story about your friend.

Word Box
good
are
friend
We

I have a _____. We like to play. _____ have

fun. We _____ _____ friends.

Who is your good friend?

_____ is my good friend!
(Write your friend's name here.)

This is a picture of my friend. (Draw a picture of your friend below.)

Match It!

Directions: Look at the pictures. Then read the sentences. Draw a line from each picture to the sentence that matches it.

1 A mother and father have a little boy.

2 Lisa and Amy are good friends.

3 A boy and girl play.

Now try this!

Draw a picture that matches this sentence:

My friend and I play.

Which Word?

Directions: Read the story. Then answer each question with a blue word from the story. We did the first one for you.

A cookie is on the bed. Will Sam sit on it? Sam sat on the cookie. Will he eat the cookie? No, but Sam's dog will be happy to eat the cookie. Sam's dog ate the cookie.

1. Which blue word ends with the letter **l**? __Will__

2. Which two blue words begins with the letter **s**?
   _____   _____

3. Which blue word rhymes with **Kate**? _____

4. Which blue word rhymes with **tree**? _____

5. Which blue word rhymes with **seat**? _____

6. Which two blue words end with the letter **e**?
   _____   _____

Match It!

Directions: Read the poem. Then choose a blue word from the poem to match each picture, below. We did the first one for you.

It rains all night, it rains all day.
The rain won't stop, we cannot play.
Look! See the sun. The day is new.
Now I want to play with you!

Look

_____

_____

_____

_____

Friends Share

Directions: Use the words in the **Word Box** to complete the story.

Word Box

for	from	with
of	If	went

Jake _____ to the zoo _____ Lilly and Sam. At the zoo, Jake had a bag _____ popcorn. The popcorn was _____ Lilly, Sam, and Jake. Lilly had popcorn _____ Jake's bag. _____ Sam wants popcorn, he can have some, too. What do you share with your friends?

Now try this!
Draw a picture of something you share with your friends.

GROUP FOUR

Go Car, Go!

Directions: Read the story. Then (circle) the word that best completes each sentence. Write the words on the lines.

Sam's father has a red car. The red car is old. It cannot

_____ fast. Sam _____ his father in
  go   goes   see   saw

the red car. It did not go. Sam's father _____
                                              want   wants

a new car.

Sam's father has a new car! The new car is green.

Sam _____ with his father in the green car. It
     go   can go

_____ fast. Sam goes in the fast green car
  go   goes

with his father.

Now try this! Write a sentence about a car.

_____

_____

This or That?

Word Box
This   new
that   old
~~book~~

Directions: Use words from the **Word Box** to fill in the blanks in the sentences below. Use the pictures to help you. We did the first one for you.

THIS   THAT

1.  This book is yellow, but that __book__ is red.

2.  This book is green, but _____ book is blue.

3. This shoe is new, but that shoe is _____.

4. This shoe is old, but that shoe is _____.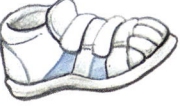

5.  _____ shoe is blue, but that shoe is red.

What Am I?

Directions: What is hidden in this picture? Follow the color words to color the picture.

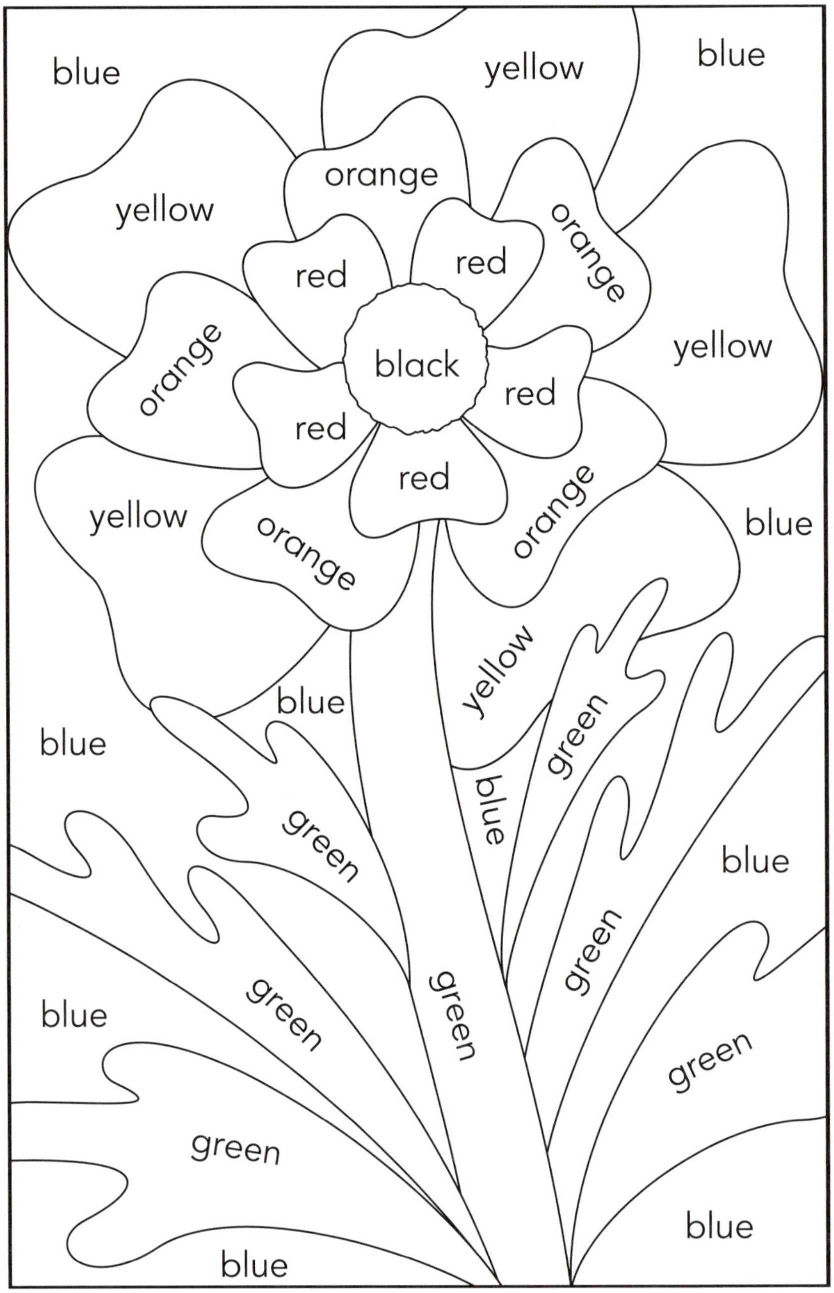

Now circle the correct answer.

I am a _____.

 flower  bird  snake

Sort It Out!

Word Box

~~blue~~	go	see
book	green	yellow
orange	red	
car	saw	

Directions: Put each word from the **Word Box** in the circle where it belongs. We did the first one for you.

THINGS

ACTIONS

COLORS
blue

Letter Detective

Directions: Read the story. Then use the letters in the **Letter Box** to complete the words below. You will use some letters more than once.

It is Jake's birthday. He wants his friends to come to his party. He will give balloons to his friends. He will get presents from his friends.

Lilly and Sam came to Jake's party. They gave presents to Jake. They got balloons from Jake. They had fun at the party.

Letter Box
a e i
o u

1 Did Lilly c _____ me to Jake's party?
Yes, she c _____ me to Jake's party.

2 Did Lilly g _____ ve a present to Jake?
Yes, she g _____ ve a present to Jake.

3 Did Lilly g _____ t a balloon from Jake?
Yes, she g _____ t a balloon from Jake.

Now try this! Which letter did you **not** use? _____

How Many?

Directions: What can you find in Jake's messy room? Look at the picture. Then answer the questions below.

Word Box

| five | one | eight | two | ten |
| seven | three | six | four | nine |

1. How many red cars are on Jake's floor? _____

2. How many fish are in Jake's fish tank? _____

3. How many blue cars are on Jake's floor? _____

4. How many dinosaurs are under Jake's chair? _____

Sparky and Lisa's Day

Directions: Read each question. Then look at the clock. Use the number words in the **Word Box** to write the correct time on the line.

Word Box
one	four	seven	ten
two	five	eight	
three	six	nine	

3 What time does Sparky meet Lisa after school?

_____ o'clock

1 What time does Sparky wake Lisa up in the morning?

_____ o'clock

4 What time does Lisa give Sparky his bath?

_____ o'clock

2 What time does Sparky take his morning walk?

_____ o'clock

Now try this!
Draw hands on the clock to show nine o'clock, Sparky and Lisa's bedtime.

Balloons for Lilly

_____ helped write this book
(Write your name here)

I read my book to:

_____ and _____ .
parent   friend

My child read this book to me.

_____   _____
parent   date

Cut along line. Fold.

circle the correct choice and write on the line. Look at the pictures for clues.

Lilly wants to go to the park. Will it rain? No, it will not ___**rain**___.

rain   run

Lilly can go ___**to**___ the park.

to   be

2

That night, Lilly is as happy as ___**as**___ she can be. It was a ___**good**___ day.

as   at

good   old

Lilly and Pete ___**sleep**___.

ran   sleep

7

Lilly goes to the park in a _____.

car can

She is with her _____. Pete

mother father

comes _____ Lilly and Mother.

with we

Lilly sees Sam. _____ is Lilly's

He She

friend. Lilly gives the green balloon

_____ Sam. _____ with the balloons.

to from   **They** We

play eat

Follow the color words to color the balloons.

A little girl **has have six seven** balloons. Lilly sees the balloons. Lilly wants one. Will she **get got** a balloon from the **boy girl**?

④

FOLD

Look! Lilly got **two four** balloons! The girl **give gave** Lilly an **orange blue** balloon and a green balloon.

⑤

If Numbers Were Walking

If numbers were walking and came in a line
You'd learn to know them in a very short time.

Oh, look over there! See, here they come!
And the first to arrive is the tall number One.

One is thin and quite straight, as suits a leader—
Now here comes Two! You know Two, don't you, reader?

Two stands good and steady on its broad base
And is curvy up top to make up its face.

Two is followed by Three, who true to its name
Is behind One and Two, who already came.

Now Four's like a house with a little steep roof
And has got a long stem leading down to its hoof.

Five is the middle, and that's where you get
When you're halfway to Ten—now don't you forget!

Let us have Six, and let it be clear
That it's one more than Five, but not Seven, my dear.

Seven is simple, it's the name that we gave
To the number that's lucky, and funny, and brave.

Eight's nothing but curves going 'round on itself
And it would fall over if it stood on a shelf.

Nine is a circle on top of a stem
And comes just before the number called Ten.

Ten is two numbers, zero after a one
And we've counted them all—now wasn't that fun?

—Samuel A. Southworth

Directions:
Listen to your teacher read this poem out loud. As you listen and read, draw a circle around each number word you find. We did the first one for you.

Notes